ADVANCED STUDIES FOR B♭ BASS

H. W. TYRRELL

1

© Copyright 1948 by Hawkes & Son (London), Ltd.; Copyright Renewed.
Copyright for all countries. All rights reserved.

Printed in U.S.A.

2

3

4

5

6

7

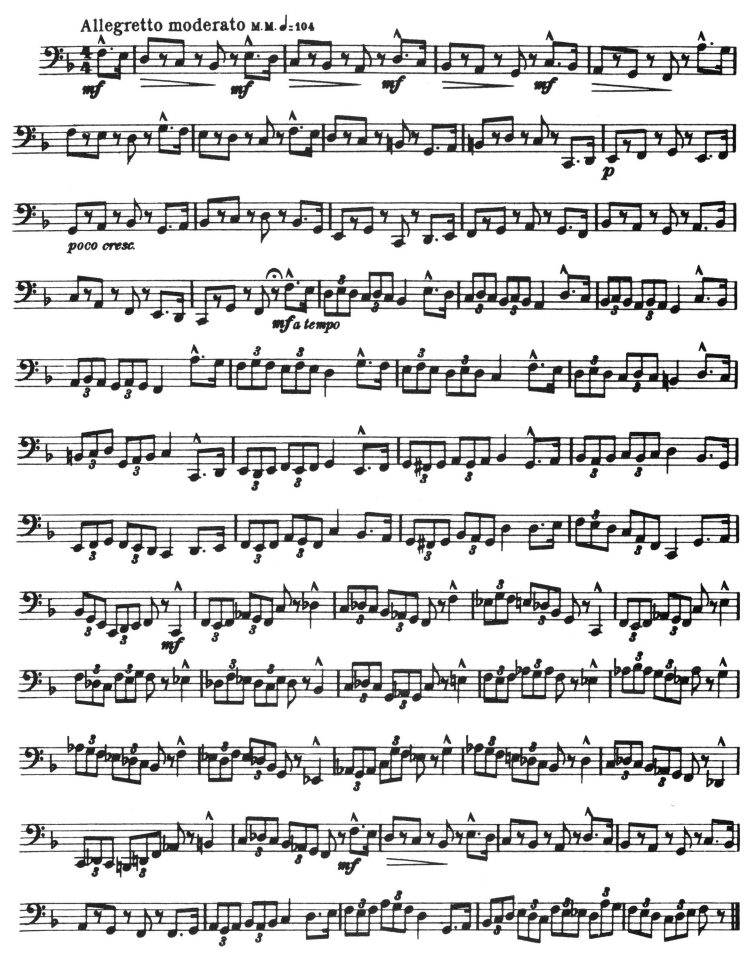

8

9

10

11

12

13

Moderato M.M. ♩ = 88

f marcato

14

15

16

17

18

19

20

21

22

23

24

25

26

27

28

29

Tempo di Polka lente M.M. ♩=80

30

31

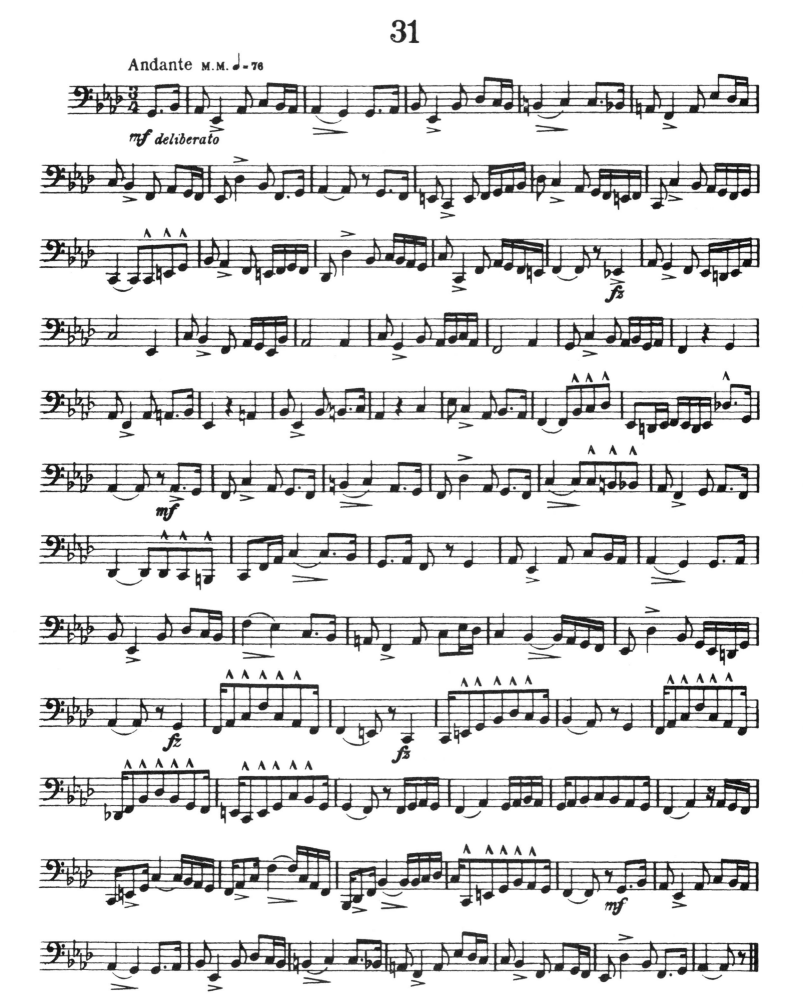

32

33

34

35

36

37

Moderato M.M. ♩ = 100

38

40

Andamento M.M. ♪ = 108
Count 8 quavers in a bar throughout

H.P. B781.7.48.